THE
ANXIETY
JOURNAL

THE ANXIETY JOURNAL

Exercises to Soothe Stress and Eliminate Anxiety Wherever You Are

CORINNE SWEET

Illustrated by
Marcia Mihotich

RODALE.

To Johnnie McKeown
with love and thanks.

INTRODUCTION

This little book will help you to identify symptoms of anxiety and will also provide you with tools and techniques to enable you to cope with them effectively. Some level of anxiety is perfectly normal – useful, even. If you're about to give a big presentation, then it would make sense for you to feel a bit jittery. But if you become fixated with anticipation, find yourself feeling sick for weeks before the date and end up staying at home because you feel so awful, then anxiety can be quite seriously detrimental. Following the advice in this book will help you to keep your anxiety at a healthy, manageable level.

Anxiety exists to make us vigilant against real-life threats; it is there for a reason, and makes us human. But for some people, living with overwhelming anxiety can feel scary or even life-threatening, and can lead to excruciating misery and suffering. Equally, low-level anxiety can cause long-term problems both at home and at work. This book won't eradicate your anxiety, as anxiety is an essential part of your emotional and physiological equipment – it keeps you alive. However, this book will help you to notice, understand and cope with your anxiety so you can begin to get on with your life and live it the way you want to. We hope *The Anxiety Journal* will help you to find a calm, peaceful place in your life.

WHAT DOES ANXIETY FEEL LIKE?

Take a moment to think about what happens to you when you feel anxious. Have you ever experienced any of the following symptoms? Feel free to circle them. Perhaps you have other symptoms too. Sometimes you can experience a symptom completely randomly, as if out of nowhere, which can be very confusing.

You might feel:

- jittery
- dizzy
- panicky
- shaky
- numb
- irritable
- cold, shivery, with goosebumps
- hypervigiliant
- as though you want to hurt yourself, or even suicidal

You might also experience:

- an inability to speak
- random, flitting thoughts
- repetitive thoughts that you can't turn off
- insomnia
- a need to sleep in the daytime
- panting
- trembling
- breathlessness or a tight chest
- a racing heart
- a dry mouth
- a clenched jaw
- clammy hands
- tingling feet or hands
- sensitive skin
- headaches or migraines
- nausea
- vomiting
- difficulty relaxing
- difficulty staying still
- a desire to excessively bite your nails or your lips, pick your scabs or scratch your skin
- sensitivity to light and sound

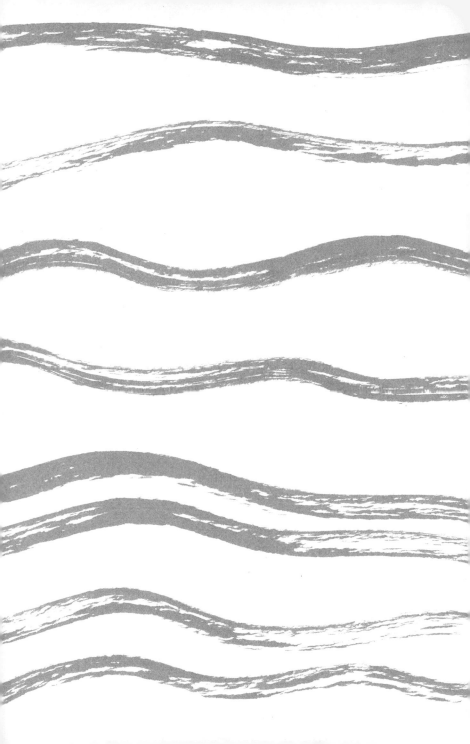

"The unexamined life is not worth living."

Socrates

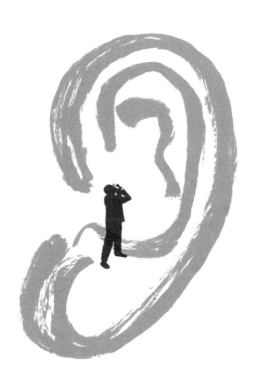

WHAT DO YOUR ANXIETY SYMPTOMS TELL YOU?

Anxiety symptoms are the body's way of warning you to "watch out." Whatever your symptoms are, and whatever order and combination they come in, they indicate a perceived threat. So what should you do when you experience such symptoms?

- Notice them
- Listen to them
- Check if the threat is real or not
- Take positive action

You don't have to live at the mercy of your anxiety, and that's where this book will help.

"It is not because things are difficult that we do not dare; it is because we do not dare that they are difficult."

Seneca

ANXIETY EPIDEMIC

We live in a stress-filled age. Stress is everywhere. Life moves faster, and thus stress seems to be on the increase. Human beings can only take so much stress before it boils over into anxiety, so it is vital to learn what your warning signs are and understand your triggers.

THE DIGITAL AGE

Ping. Beep. Bzzz. We are tied to our devices night and day. Stress is often prompted by the use of social media, which makes many people feel they are missing out if they are not partying 24/7 or do not have the perfect body, a wonderful love life and a jet-set career . . .

It's easy to look at social media pages, such as Facebook, Instagram, Snapchat and LinkedIn, and feel like you are "less than," which increases your anxiety.

Recent research has shown that over 55 percent of people have negative reactions to looking at pictures of others online, as they evoke feelings of jealousy, envy, low self-esteem and competitiveness. We are expected to keep up with the latest viral sensations and live news reports. We are exposed to twenty-four-hour news reports of disasters and death, and this exposure heightens anxiety.

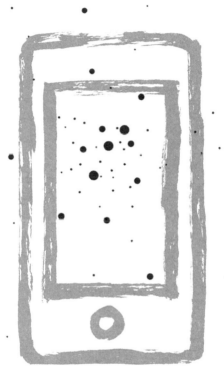

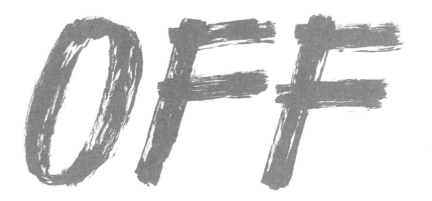

TAKE POWER

Remember you can turn off your devices. You can take a break. Take time out to slow things down. Stop tweeting, stop checking.

You can do this whenever you want to.

Give yourself a "digi-break" of an hour or, even better, half a day. Turn off your devices and instead put your attention on the people in your present: your friends, your colleagues, your family, your neighbors, your cat or dog – all who surround you all the time, in real time, in your life.

ACCEPTANCE

What we do in the face of the anxiety epidemic is key
to how we learn to handle our lives and our reactions to
pressure. Accept that pressure is a given – it is not going to
go away. In fact, it will probably increase as life gets faster
and more demanding – and thus you need to find a new
way of dealing with it to keep yourself calm and sane.

Experiment: spend half a day, or a whole day, not listening
to news or reading the paper or checking online data.
Just give yourself a break: notice the sky, the colors on
your street, wildlife. Try tuning out for a while and see how
it feels.

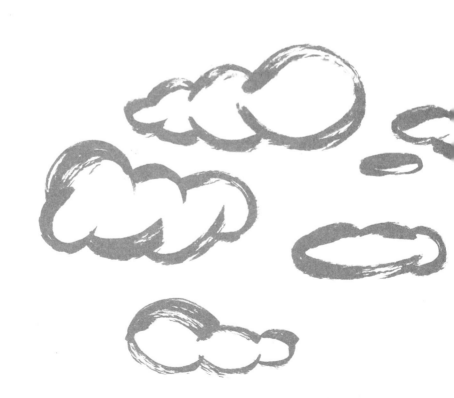

SURROUND YOURSELF WITH WARMTH

Anxiety is infectious, especially if you are already in a vulnerable place.

Try this:

Take a moment. Close your eyes and think of a person – a good friend or your partner, perhaps.

Do you get an "up" warm feeling when you think of them? Or do you get a "down" cold feeling? Notice your reactions. If they are cold or heavy, limit your contact, even if you care for them. It's important to learn how others affect you – and to protect yourself, thoughtfully. If you feel like you've had enough of someone, then you probably have.

Do you really want to conquer your anxiety? Even if it involves you changing your habits, challenging your way of thinking, behaving and responding? Or even changing your friends and contacts?

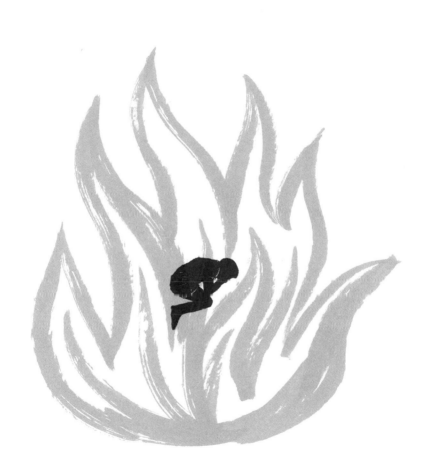

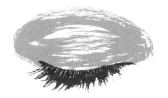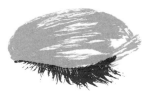

A SIMPLE CALMING EXERCISE

Find a quiet spot in your house or workplace where you can sit and be comfortable on your own for five minutes.

Close your eyes and breathe deeply in and out.

Notice where the tension lies in your body: your belly, your back, neck, head, jaw . . . where?

Just notice and breathe deeply, in and out, five times.

Breathe into the places that feel tense, and imagine them melting, like soft butter or marshmallows in heat . . .

Then open your eyes, stretch like a cat and go on with your day.

TRIGGERS

Everyone will have triggers that set off their anxiety.
You can think of them as early-warning buttons – once
they are pressed, they can lead to stress.

Sometimes we imagine things are scarier or more
dangerous than they are, often as a result of our past
experiences, and we get triggered unnecessarily.

Notice the places where you get anxious. Is it walking
along a street in the dark at night? Sitting in traffic? Being
alone at home?

Things are often more benign than we realize, but we
get upset because we let our fear take over our common
sense.

When you feel anxious, ask yourself: am I truly in danger
or do I just think I am?

Take a moment to think about your own triggers:

- What sets off your anxiety?
- Do you see any regular patterns?
- Do you notice your early warning symptoms?

We explore triggers further later on in the book, but just
note what comes to mind now.

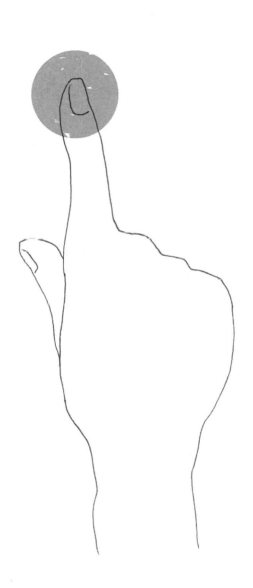

"The greatest discovery of my generation is that a human being can alter his life by altering his attitudes of mind."

William James

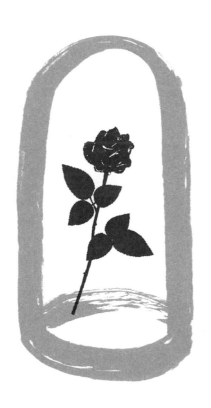

WHAT'S IN A NAME?

Words associated with anxiety and anxious people are often quite derogatory. Society values people being "brave," "strong" or able to "cope" and tends to put down those who feel fearful or show their vulnerabilities.

Women are often caricatured as being less strong, so "being a girl" or "girly" condemns them for feeling frightened or anxious about something (never mind the sexist implications of attempting to insult a man by associating him with supposedly feminine tendencies).

If you are anxious, or show your anxiety openly, other people can make all sorts of assumptions about the kind of person you are, often negatively. You no doubt already know that life with anxiety can be difficult but consider this: people who suffer from anxiety are often blessed with personality traits that non-anxious people are not. They tend to be more sensitive, creative, imaginative, responsive and intuitive, and contribute a great deal to the world that is valuable. Artists, writers, actors, musicians, inventors, designers, innovators, scientists, composers, psychologists, therapists, healers, doctors and many more are often perceptive and aware, and what people would call "anxious"… It's no bad thing.

ANXIETY ALCHEMY

Anxiety tends to be described negatively, even derogatorily, but such labels are unhelpful and pessimistic. There's no getting around the fact that chronic anxiety is incredibly difficult to live with, but it's important not to let it damage your self-esteem.

How might the negative descriptions below be considered positive traits? Consider your own personality, your own anxiety, and add descriptions that can apply to you.

For example:

Worrier > Attentive to detail
Hyper > Energetic
Frightened > Careful

Now try it yourself. Think of some words people use to describe your anxiety symptoms, and turn them into positive characteristics.

As much as possible, try to implement this optimistic viewpoint in your day-to-day life, whether it's others' attitudes or your own that are getting you down.

Anxiety words . . .

"As a man thinks, so does he become. Every man is the son of his own works."

Miguel de Cervantes

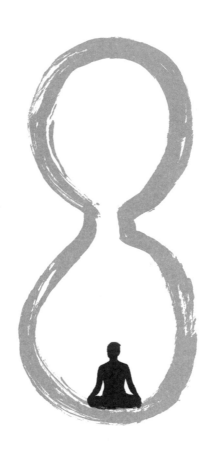

FIVE MINUTE DE-STRESS EXERCISE

Set a timer for five minutes.

Sit comfortably in a quiet place and notice your thoughts.

Close your eyes and visualize them as ping-pong balls, pinging off the walls. See them bouncing around, buzzing away from one topic to another . . .

Focus on your breathing. Breathe in and out, and notice your thoughts, but don't follow them, let them go. Let them bounce out of view, out of the room, one by one.

Keep breathing. Bring your attention back to just behind your forehead, in the middle, and let your thoughts calm, noticing them retreating, and don't pay them any attention.

Keep breathing and actively notice your chest and abdomen rising as you breathe in and falling as you breathe out.

Think "rising" as you breathe in, "falling" as you breathe out.

When the timer goes off, open your eyes slowly. Notice where you are.

Breathe and be aware that you feel less stressed now.

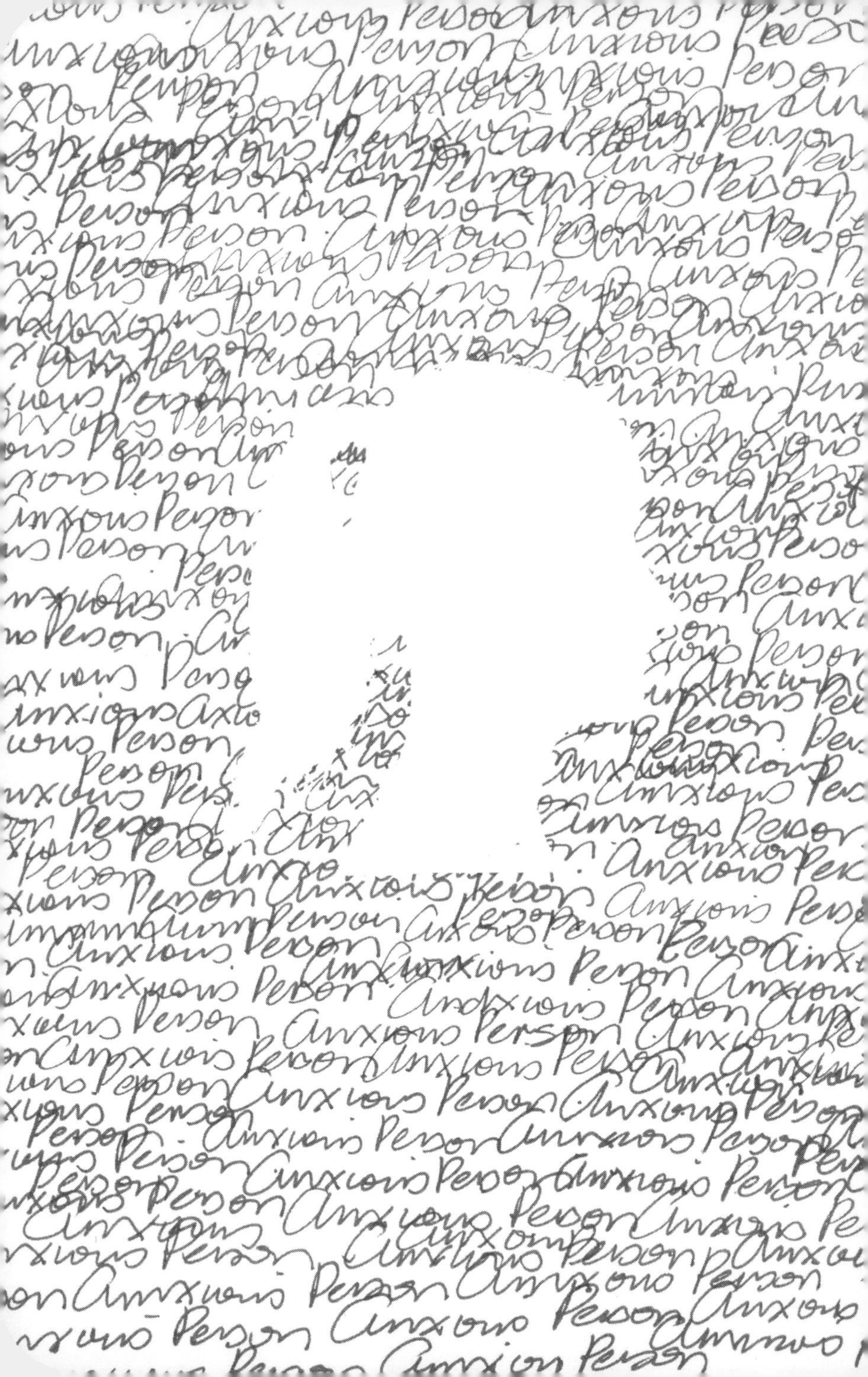

SEPARATE PEOPLE FROM
THEIR PATTERNS

It's important to separate people from their patterns.
And that includes you.

Don't think, *She's an anxious person,* and disregard the rest
of her. Think, *Suzie suffers from anxiety – but she's a great
friend/cook/dancer.*

Do the same for yourself – don't dismiss yourself as
"anxious" and therefore useless. Make a distinction
between your anxiety symptoms and yourself – you
are far more capable than you probably give yourself
credit for.

You are a person first and the fact that you contain
patterns is a secondary matter.

GOOD STRESS AND BAD STRESS

Good stress is the right amount of energy and attention you need to get something done. A boost of adrenaline and off you go, you get the task finished on time. Good stress can aid productivity and achievement.

Bad stress occurs when you feel overloaded or when you have too many conflicting demands and feel torn in too many directions all at once. Bad stress makes you feel overwhelmed and might actually make you ill. Bad stress makes you feel, ultimately, a failure.

We all need to learn to distinguish between the good stress and the bad stress in our lives and to emphasize and develop the good parts, while eliminating the bad ones.

Stress is a given. Stress is here to stay. Stress is endemic. Stress is life. It's how we anticipate it, tackle it and live with it, transform it, which will make all the difference.

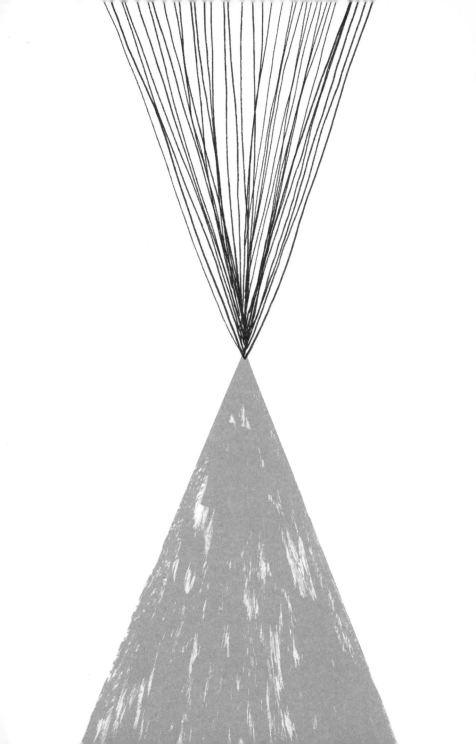

"You can't stop the waves, but you can learn to surf."

Jon Kabat-Zinn

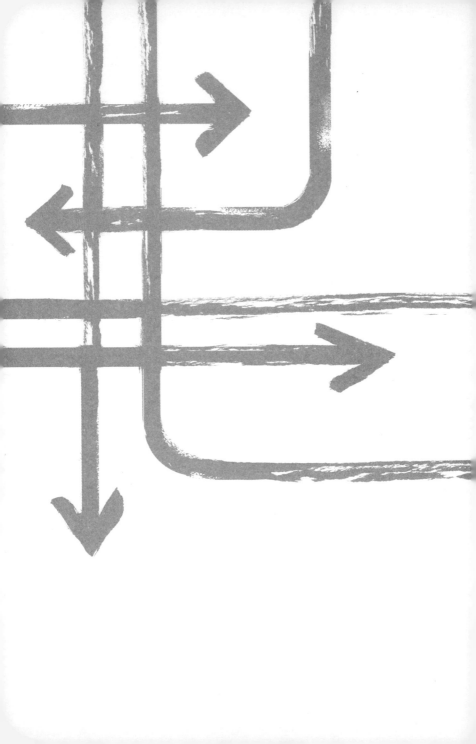

Anxiety-prone people often ask "what if." "What if I take the highway and there's a crash?" "What if . . ."

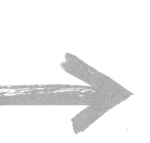

ANXIETY MINDSET

If you have an anxiety mindset, you constantly turn over issues, thinking about the future, picking over the past, constantly analyzing, worrying, or nit-picking about what did happen or might happen. It's exhausting and, ultimately, unproductive.

Anxiety-prone people often ask "what if." "What if I take the highway and there's a crash?" "What if it rains and I get wet? I might get pneumonia and die?" "What if I say something stupid?" This kind of anxiety is largely fear of the unknown, of taking risks and of feeling unprepared or unable to deal with the unseen.

Another common phrase is "If only...." "If only we'd gotten up earlier, we wouldn't have been delayed." Or "If only I had a million dollars, then I wouldn't have any money worries." "If only I hadn't eaten that cake, I wouldn't have got sick/put on weight." This kind of anxiety is tinged with regret and often disguises anger and resentment.

The third anxiety mindset is "shoulda, coulda, woulda." This kind of anxiety mindset is about what you should have done, what could have been and what would have happened. This is the worst kind of negative mindset, as it is a major way of beating yourself up for the past, the present and the future.

This mindset takes a huge amount of energy and can become quite obsessive, as we worry away trying to rewrite history. "I should have gotten up early, and then we could have caught that train and we would have seen the Queen... It's ruined the whole day, ruined the whole vacation." Shoulda, coulda, woulda can also be a passive-aggressive way of blaming other people. Either way, it usually erases positive thinking as you constantly try and change the past and the future, without being able to live in the present.

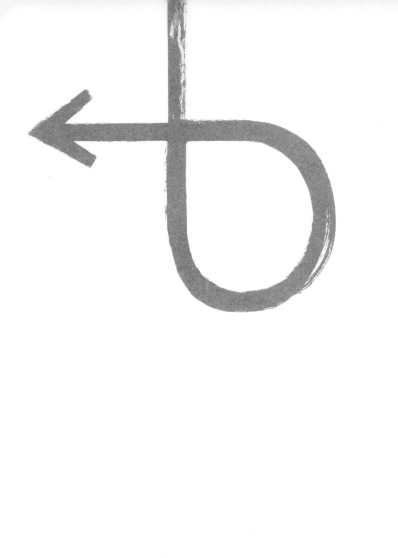

LEAVING THE ANXIETY
MINDSET BEHIND

The anxiety mindset is particularly common if you grew up with anxious parents, have experienced a lot of trauma in your life, or have had some bad experiences without good support. Or maybe you are just made that way. But you can end up using a lot of valuable energy worrying about things before they actually happen.

This can make you miserable as well as making other people exhausted and annoyed. It is also just a bad habit really and can be given up. It's something you can learn to conquer – if you want to. The key is to learn to catch yourself when you start off on a path toward anxiety.

Consider your own mind. Are you a "what if," "if only" or "shoulda, woulda, coulda" thinker? Perhaps you're all three. Try to take notice the next time you embark on this sort of thinking. Don't beat yourself up about it. Instead, try to just be aware when you do it.

Catch yourself.

Then, gently correct yourself, and gradually you can learn to nip it in the bud and stay calm before it escalates out of control.

It's all about unlearning a bad habit and replacing it with something new so that you can leave the anxiety mindset behind.

"The secret of life is balance, and the absence of balance is life's destruction."

Hazrat Inayat Khan

ANXIETY SPIRAL

Anxiety can spiral out of control very easily. Once you feel anxious about one thing, all the other things start spinning too, making it easy to spiral down into an anxiety whirlpool where you worry about absolutely anything and everything. This can often happen in the middle of the night.

So, the anxiety spiral is an important habit to unlearn.

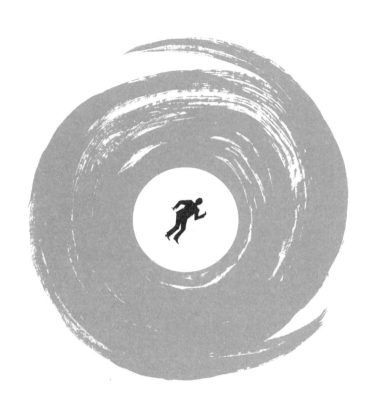

SPIRAL STAIRCASE

Imagine you are on a spiral staircase, going down, down, down into the dark. You don't like it. Halfway down you want to get off, but you can't go back up, and you don't want to go further down.

Someone throws you a rope. You catch it and you are towed up to the light and the fresh air. Freedom.

This is a useful mental picture you can use to stop being anxious.

You need to catch yourself going down and take a fresh step, hold on to the rope and move upward finding a new sense of yourself and your inner strength.

Stop yourself going down, round and round. Make a decision to stop, to get off and not to go there. If you struggle to control your thought patterns, try one of the relaxation exercises in this book to distract yourself.

It is important to remember you can decide to change your mood – it is your choice.

SOCIAL ANXIETY

Some people feel very anxious when meeting people or going into social situations. You are not alone. Most of us feel some level of shyness, or awkwardness, when meeting someone new. It's quite natural. However, sometimes these feelings can become overwhelming and actually stop us living our lives to the fullest.

Social anxiety often comes from being hurt by people in the past, perhaps through being teased or bullied. It is important to try and understand what has made you shy with people, so you can do something about it.

Some people are hardwired to find social contact difficult and may be on the autistic spectrum (this can be diagnosed). For many people, it comes back to a feeling of inadequacy or low self-esteem: a belief that no one will talk to you, or if they do, they will find you boring or you won't be able to think of anything to say. Or you might feel self-conscious and awkward, unable to be comfortable in your own skin.

If you have social anxiety, you can end up making decisions based on not having to interact with people. You might avoid going to a party or out for a drink with friends. Or you might not apply for a job for fear of messing up the interview. And dating seems out of the question.

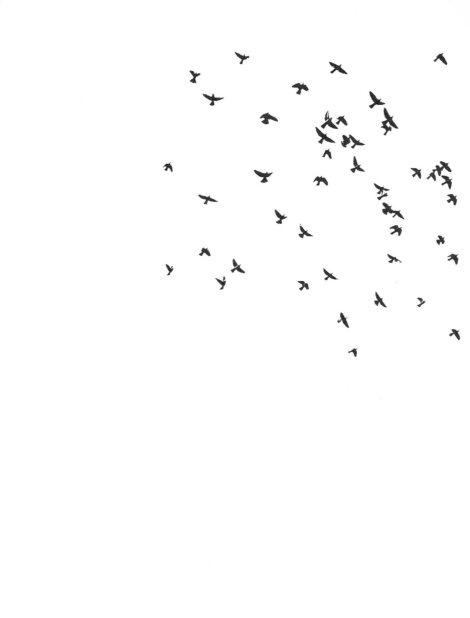

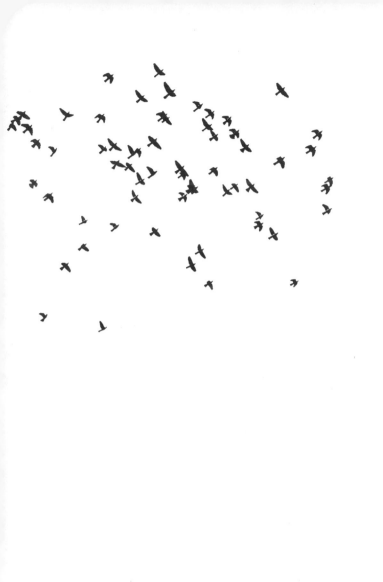

Sometimes people with social anxiety live online, as they feel safer there. This is a good place to start but real, face-to-face contact will give you so much more, especially longer term.

The good news is that social anxiety is understood now more than ever. You don't have to hide all your anxious feelings, and you can admit to feeling shy or awkward. It can actually be endearing, as it makes the other person feel OK about their shy feelings too.

"Your anxiety and fears are not you and . . . they do not have to rule your life."

Jon Kabat-Zinn

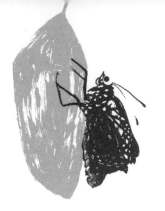

THE CHANGE PARADOX

Being anxious is intrinsically linked to our survival instincts, so it can be difficult to contemplate giving it up. Yet always feeling worried, anxious, panicky and nervous about things can make you miserable.

Some clients say to me, "I want to be less anxious."

To which I reply, "So what would you like to do to change your anxiety?"

The response is often, "But I hate change," and what they really mean is, "I want to change . . . just as long as I don't really have to make changes."

I call this the change paradox. If you want to feel less anxious all the time, if you want to give up feeling nervous and at the mercy of your fear, you will need to make a decision to actively change your behaviour and your thought processes.

Change will involve doing something new, amending your habits, developing new ways of thinking and creating a new way of being. It's about holding your own hand while you do something that scares you. These are not quick fixes and the process might involve making some sacrifices.

Take a moment to honestly consider whether the change paradox is true of you. Do you hold yourself back? Do you trip yourself up? Are you hard on yourself?

HOLD ON

Hold your own hand, in a clasp.

Feel how solid your hands feel together. Feel the strength.
You are with yourself.

Solid and dependable. You are enough, in yourself, for
you to hold on to.

If there is something you want to change, you can do it.
You just have to see that you have enough strength
in yourself.

Just hold your own hand, and you can do it.

Right here. Right now.

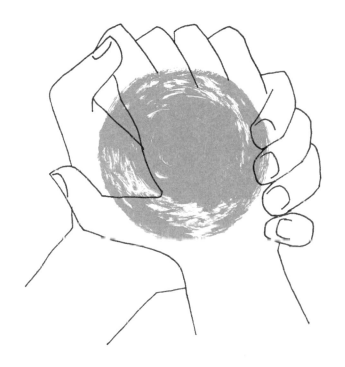

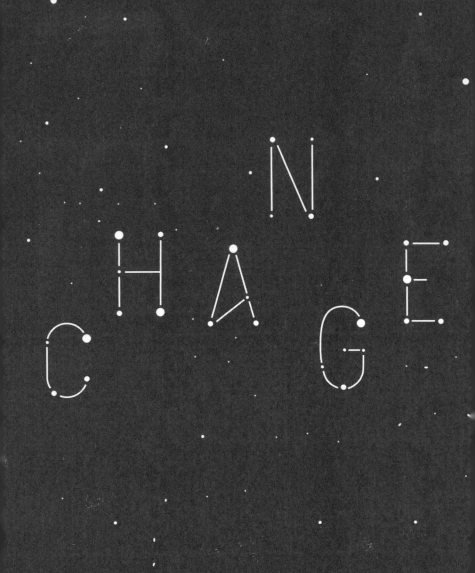

FEAR OF CHANGE

Do you fear what would happen if you gave up worrying?

Sometimes people talk about their anxiety as if they are talking about their best friend. Something they are loathe to let go of. "I'm just made this way" is common, or "I am a nervous person, that's just how I am." It's true that we are all individual, with individual ways, but sometimes embracing change can feel like a threat.

Remember, though: even if you make drastic changes to your life to combat your anxiety, you will always be you . . . But you could be a calmer version of you, more able to function in a crisis, more able to cope with the unknown and less hindered and exhausted by fear

You can only learn to grasp and outwit your own change paradox (if you have one) by deciding to change for yourself.

Make a promise to yourself, right here, right now, that you will make changes.

"Considering how dangerous everything is, nothing is really very frightening."

Gertrude Stein

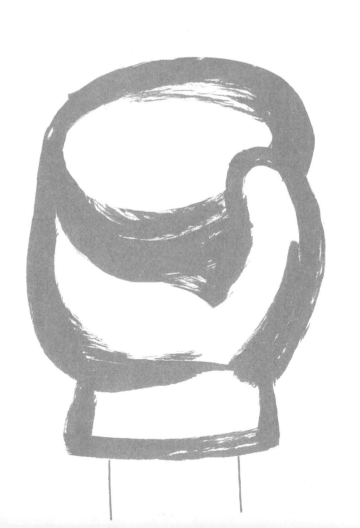

WHAT IS ANXIETY FOR?

We are all hardwired with complex neurophysiological reactions to danger. When we are under threat, our autonomic nervous system leaps into action. Hormones from the endocrine system are released and our hearts work faster, palpitating in order to oxygenate our blood. Our kidneys secrete adrenaline and cortisol into the bloodstream so that our muscles can work faster and our limbs can work harder for longer. Before we have a chance to think, we react in one of three ways:

- fight
- flight
- freeze

These physiological reactions might make us feel stronger – more able to fight or run away. Alternatively, we might hold our breath and freeze. In this case, our minds are racing, pumped up on the adrenaline and cortisol, but we are so over-pumped or shocked that time slows down, or even stands still, as we tense every muscle to stay motionless.

What are your experiences? Have you ever felt threatened or been in danger? How did your body react? How did your mind react? What did you do? How did you feel afterward?

Notes

Notes

"We are healed from suffering only by experiencing it to the full."

Marcel Proust

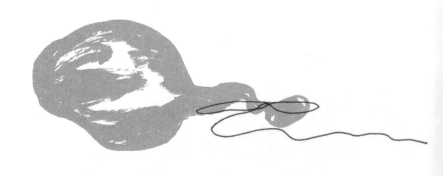

ANXIETY AFTERMATH

After experiencing the flight, fight or freeze response, due to perceived threat or actual danger, there is usually a "cooldown," when the body has to process all the biochemical reactions to danger and when the brain deals with what has just happened.

There can be an overload of chemicals in the blood, meaning the body has to readjust to get back to normal, so this can lead to anxiety aftermath. This manifests itself in a number of ways such as feeling jittery, sweaty, unable to sleep or very sleepy, unable to eat or very hungry or irritable or withdrawn. It might come on immediately after your anxiety episode or hours, days or even longer afterward.

Your physiological and emotional response depends on how long the threat lasted, whether it was brief (like being threatened on the street) or sustained (such as being in an abusive relationship), and whether it was avoided or it was actually experienced.

You need to remember that what goes up must come down. Even in the midst of feeling fear, and its aftermath, you will feel fine again later.

ALL WILL BE WELL

One way to remind yourself of this, in the midst of feeling jittery, is to close your eyes, briefly, and think of a good, benign object: a flower, your cat, your child, an ocean shore, a tree, a lovely walk, a sunset.

Breathe, imagining the image.

All will be well, breathe and relax.

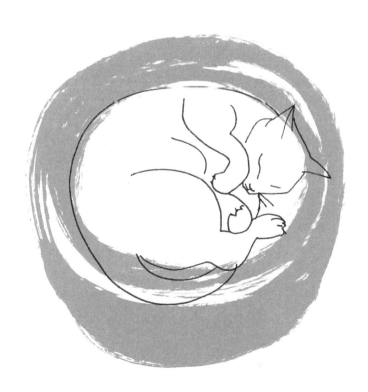

DREAMS

Anxiety aftermath can cause disturbed sleep and provoke unsettling dreams. You may have nightmares, night sweats and repetitive dreams as your brain tries to process your fear. You might have an anxiety dream before a specific event like a job interview, a first date, or when moving in to a new house. Or you might have one after a frightening event or episode. Dreams are your mind's way of processing the experience and making sense of the emotions that have been stirred.

You might find it helpful to keep a dream diary to monitor how you are processing fear – is the process conscious or not?

If you wake up anxious in the night, try talking into your phone to record your thoughts, as it often helps release fear to speak it out loud.

Writing down your fears, or speaking them out loud, can help you get back to peaceful sleep.

"Our anxiety does not come from thinking about the future but from wanting to control it."

Kahlil Gibran

TRAUMA

If you have witnessed or experienced physical, emotional or sexual abuse, death, disaster or crime, an accident or an injury, you may experience a very high level of anxiety that continues for a long time and becomes a trauma.

If you are traumatized, you emotionally re-experience the terrible thing that happened again and again in order to make sense of it, and there are many symptoms that come with this process. One major symptom of trauma is heightened anxiety, which can become chronic over time.

Consider whether a trauma from the past might be contributing to your anxiety.

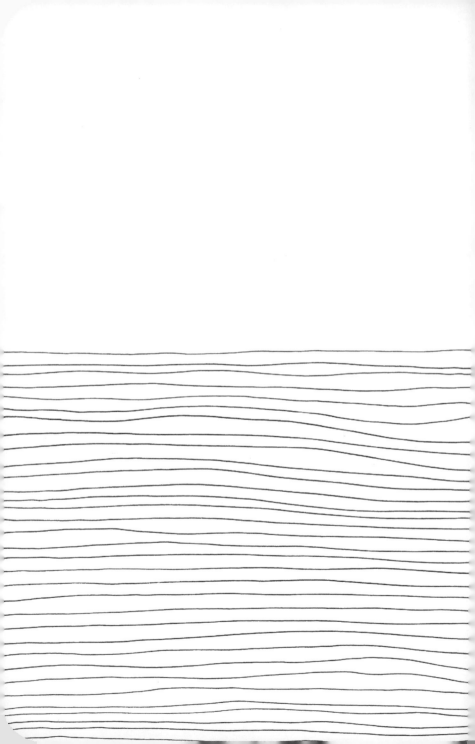

SOOTHING YOUR TRAUMA

Lie down or sit comfortably. Set your timer for ten minutes.

Close your eyes. Breathe in three times, slowly and deeply.

Take your mind to a lovely, peaceful place you have experienced, such as a beautiful garden or a seashore.

Imagine yourself walking through the garden, looking at the flowers; or walking along the shore, toes sinking into the sand. As you walk, notice the blooms, the colors; or the sea, the sky, the colors. Imagine yourself walking, calming as you do, with the sun on your back, taking in the lovely surroundings.

Carry on walking in your mind's eye, and continue to breathe slowly and deeply.

Keep bringing your mind back to the beautiful, benign scene.

When the timer goes off, open your eyes slowly.

CHRONIC ANXIETY

Chronic anxiety occurs when you are unable to cut the cycle of fear and you perceive danger everywhere. It's like a red alert button that is stuck in the On position and causes your kidneys, heart and other organs to constantly pump out biochemicals to combat a real or imagined threat, putting your brain and body under unrelenting stress as a consequence.

It's vitally important not to underestimate the effect that chronic anxiety can have on your health, both short-term (e.g. breathing difficulties, the development of asthma, high blood pressure, addiction) and long-term (e.g. chronic fatigue syndrome, heart failure, kidney failure, cancers).

Chronic anxiety can also lead to obsessive tendencies or obsessive compulsive disorder (OCD), which can seriously inhibit your life. You might get frightened of going outside (agoraphobia), of being too enclosed (claustrophobia) or of being up too high (vertigo).

Additionally, if the thoughts and feelings become too overwhelming, for too long, and are accompanied by lack of sleep, it can feel tempting to consider suicide or self-harm in order to gain some inner peace, control and final release.

It is incredibly important not to put up with anxiety but to start to take action at the first sign of symptoms. We've looked at the differences between good and bad anxiety. If your anxiety has not yet become chronic, then take steps to nip it in the bud.

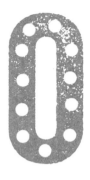
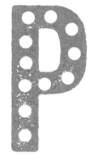
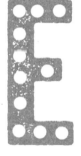
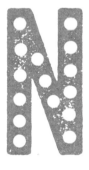

HELP IS AT HAND

There is no shame in getting help. Share your fears
with someone trusted, like a friend, doctor or a family
member. It is perfectly possible to calm chronic anxiety,
but it does take effort. The first place to start is to decide
to get help. Reach out to someone. Put yourself first. You
are not alone.

It is particularly important to seek professional help if you
are struggling through chronic anxiety.

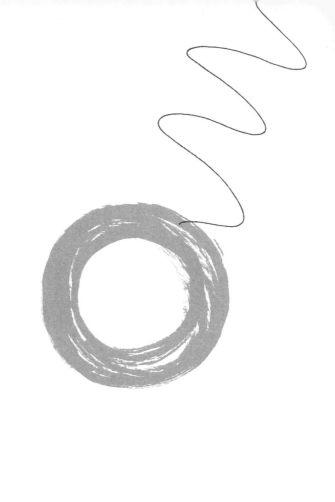

"Let us be grateful to people who make us happy, they are the charming gardeners who make our souls blossom."

Marcel Proust

SEE A DOCTOR AND/OR THERAPIST

If you are experiencing physical symptoms and physiological changes which worry you, see a doctor or find an alternative health therapist. Seeing a physician usually offers a reality check. You might find an alternative health practitioner is more open to understanding the psychological aspects of your physical symptoms, as they are trained to look at you holistically, so they will take into account your emotional state as well as your physical well-being.

If you are particularly anxious about being ill, you may be suffering from hypochondria (aka health anxiety), which is an anxiety-based condition. You should seek psychological help to deal with this and would do well to try therapy.

You may find that seeing an alternative health practitioner will suit you – acupuncture, acupressure, reiki and reflexology are just a few treatments that can help you relax.

There is no shame in seeing a therapist. We all need someone to talk to confidentially from time to time, and talking will help relieve anxiety and bodily stress.

Remember that in China the barefoot doctors are paid to keep people well, not paid when they get ill. It is a great reversal of Western thinking: we need to invest in our wellness rather than our illness, and only you are able to take control of that.

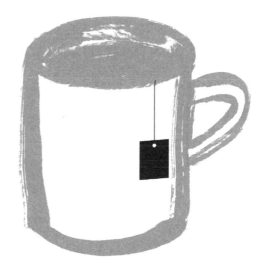

"What does not kill me makes me stronger."

Friedrich Nietzsche

SECONDARY TRAUMATIZATION

There is a growing body of psychological, physiological and scientific evidence that our hectic, pressured 24/7 lifestyles are doing us immense harm. Not least, the constant media saturation that we experience through TV, radio and social media means that many of us never turn off.

Live reporting of distressing news, such as bombings, wars, murders, accidents, natural disasters and so on, raise our individual anxiety levels. In a sense, many of us experience secondary traumatization, for even if we are nowhere near the action, our own anxiety responses are triggered, leading to the fight, flight, freeze responses and therefore to potential chronic anxiety.

The problem with media saturation is that many of us feel, understandably, that the world is not a safe place, that there are attackers on every street corner and that we are under constant threat simply because we see this happening all the time on our devices.

In fact, most experts believe we are safer than ever, despite what the media leads us to feel and believe. There are actually fewer wars, fewer murders, and more security. It is just that what happens is better publicized, so our senses are overloaded and create a greater, ongoing feeling of threat.

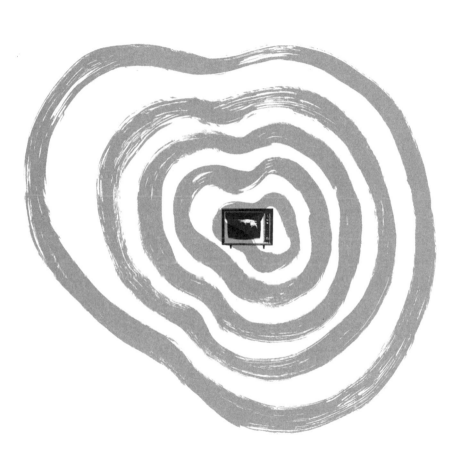

GOOD NEWS STORY

Take a newspaper or go to your favorite news website. How many positive news stories are there? Make a note of them. Now make a note of all the good things you see or hear about that happen today, whether it's as small as someone making faces at a child on the bus or perhaps something bigger: a colleague's new baby or an award for a local hero. I bet you'll run out of paper.

Good news stories . . .

"The greatest griefs are those we cause ourselves."

Sophocles

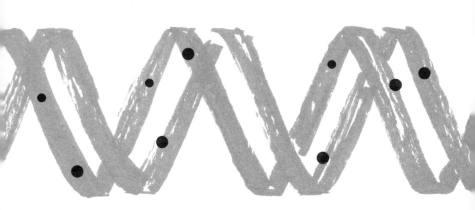

GENERALIZED ANXIETY DISORDER

Generalized Anxiety Disorder is the medical term for a condition that causes you to feel anxious about a wide range of situations and issues rather than one specific (traumatic or other) event.

How anxious you get is based on three main things. Firstly, your genes and DNA (nature). You may come from a family which is more reactive to stimuli than other people (as not all human beings are the same).

Secondly, anxiety can be learned (nurture). If your parents or relatives were highly sensitive to certain things, it's possible that this will impact on you. You might feel threatened in similar circumstances. These anxiety patterns can be handed down.

Thirdly, your reactions are influenced by cultural and environmental differences. If you grew up in a war, in economic difficulty, in an oppressed community or have lived through a disaster or a traumatic situation, this will influence your reactions. Being in a crowd can exacerbate anxiety, and even lead to panic.

Generalized Anxiety Disorder really means your anxiety button is switched on all the time. It can lead to obsessive thinking, extreme thoughts and unnecessary avoidance of perceived danger.

However, even if you feel anxious about a lot of things, a lot of the time you can still do something about lowering your anxiety for yourself.

ANXIETY AND MEDICATION

If you feel your anxiety is overwhelming or you are
chronically anxious, you can go to your doctor to get
medication or talk with a therapist about taking
some medication to help with your anxiety. It is important
to deal with the symptoms as they become too distressing.
Sometimes there is need for them to be alleviated while
you work out what to change in your life, or you may
be going through a situation like a divorce, addiction
recovery or a layoff that puts you under pressure
for a long time.

However, there is an increasing body of evidence,
recognized by NICE (the National Institute for Health
and Care Excellence), that there are other, non-medical
ways of dealing with the physical and psychological
symptoms of anxiety. These methods include
mindfulness, CBT, alternative health therapies and
talking therapies. Your doctor should discuss these with
you, and you can always ask for a referral yourself.

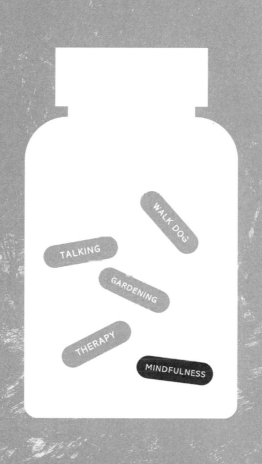

"Our life is what our thoughts make it."

Marcus Aurelius

PANIC ATTACKS

Sometimes extreme anxiety can strike when you are least expecting it. Panic attacks can be triggered either by something in your mind (such as a memory or a perception), something in your environment (like feeling under threat or being in real danger) or by something you perceive before you consciously notice it (a smell or a sound). You might start panicking before you are consciously aware of, or understand, the trigger.

Typical symptoms of a panic attack include but are not limited to: panting and feeling that you are not able to breathe; numbness in the face and limbs; tingling of the hands and/or feet; a feeling of unreality; feeling sick or actual vomiting; a need to get out of a place very quickly, to escape; an overwhelming sense of dread, of overpowering fear; sweating, either hot or cold, or both; clammy hands and skin; dry mouth; needing to go to the toilet, or actually doing so; blankness, feeling unable to think.

Panic attacks can come in waves. If you experience one attack, you may experience several in close proximity and this in itself can be very distressing. Indeed, much as you can have anxiety about your anxiety, you can panic about panicking.

The only way to deal with panic is to learn to nip it in the bud. You need to recognize your triggers and avoid or handle them effectively.

IDENTIFYING TRIGGERS

Jot down things you notice that trigger you. It could be strobe lights or the taste of a particular food, a crowded train or loud noises or a type of dog. If you write these things down, you can remind yourself you are sensitive to them, and you can either avoid these things/situations, or deal with them with awareness, should you be confronted with them.

Learning what your triggers are is an important part of conquering your panic.

Then you need to find out what to do if panic has already set in – the sooner you handle it, the better.

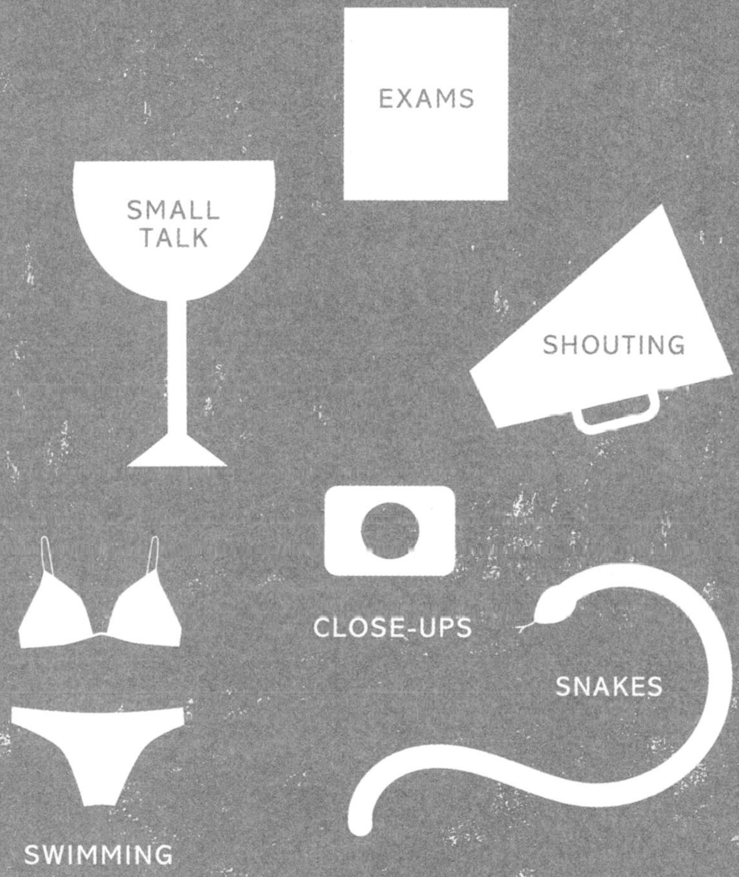
EXAMS
SMALL TALK
SHOUTING
CLOSE-UPS
SNAKES
SWIMMING

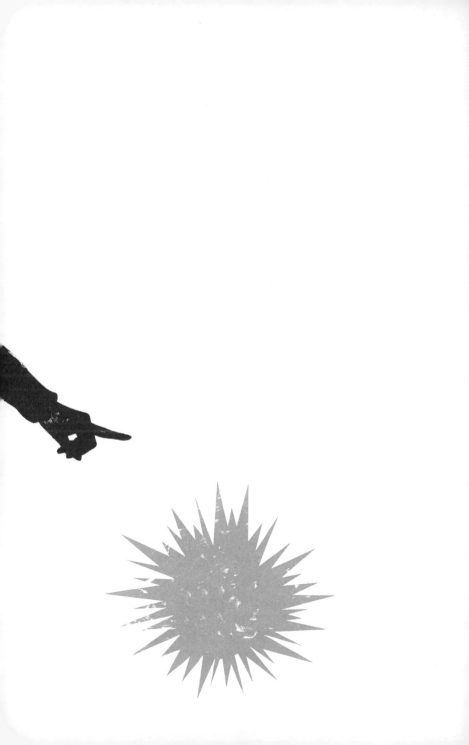

HANDLING PANIC

Breathe. You may feel you can't, but you can.

Slow down your breathing.

Count to ten slowly in your mind: one, two, three, four, and so on.

Breathe slowly in and out as you continue counting, then start counting backward: ten, nine, eight, seven, etc.

Tell yourself you will survive. It is just fear, just feelings, and it will pass.

Understanding your triggers and learning to handle your panic, if you get an attack, will take you much further and be much more effective in breaking the escalation of anxiety and panic, long term. The information and exercises on the next few pages will help you to do this.

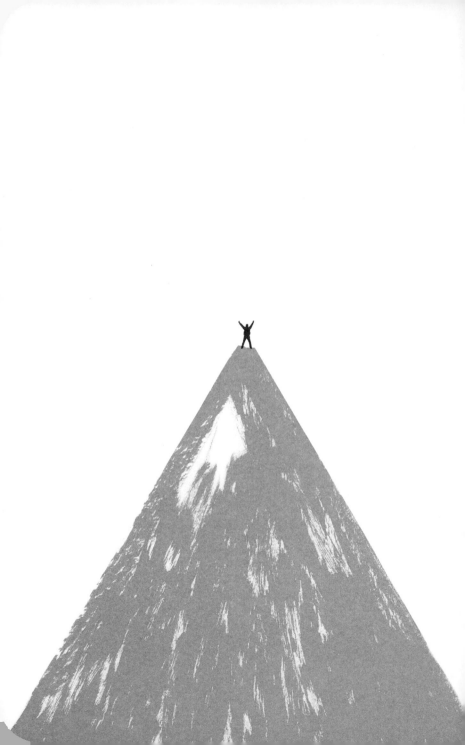

CONQUERING PANIC

If you have never had a panic attack before, it can take you by surprise. In fact, even if you've had a hundred, they can still feel terrifying. Try these tips for reducing panic:

1) **Familiarize yourself**, if you can, with your usual symptoms that signal an attack – the more you understand your triggers the better prepared you will be.

2) **Understand that you are safe!** Even though you are feeling panicky, you are, in reality, safe and there is no need to be frightened. You won't die even if you feel terrified.

3) **Breathe.** Concentrate on your breathing. Blow out slowly. Then breathe in and blow out again, to the count of ten. Do this several times, breathing deeper each time (but try not to hyperventilate). Slow your breathing, and breathe more shallowly, if you start feeling dizzy or light-headed.

4) **Stamp your feet** on the ground. Feel how solid it is.

5) **Hold something** like the arm of a chair, a bannister, even your own hand.

6) **Tell yourself,** "I can do this. I can get through this. This will pass."

7) Count slowly from one to ten, and then from ten to one.

8) Slow down your walking, stop driving or leave the room, the bus, the train and breathe some air. Don't rush, but get yourself some space.

9) If the feelings continue, try singing (especially in a private space like a car or your home or in the toilet), just 'La la la" or something simple like a nursery rhyme or favorite song. Loud singing can make you feel cheerful and cut the panic pattern.

10) Take a walk. Even if it's just to the other end of your office or room, but ideally outside somewhere.

11) Continue breathing. Stretch your fingers and toes, breathe deeply. Congratulate yourself for getting through what felt life-threatening – and notice three nice things in your environment (a pot plant, red shoes, the sky, etc.).

"We could never learn to be brave and patient if there were only joy in the world."

Helen Keller

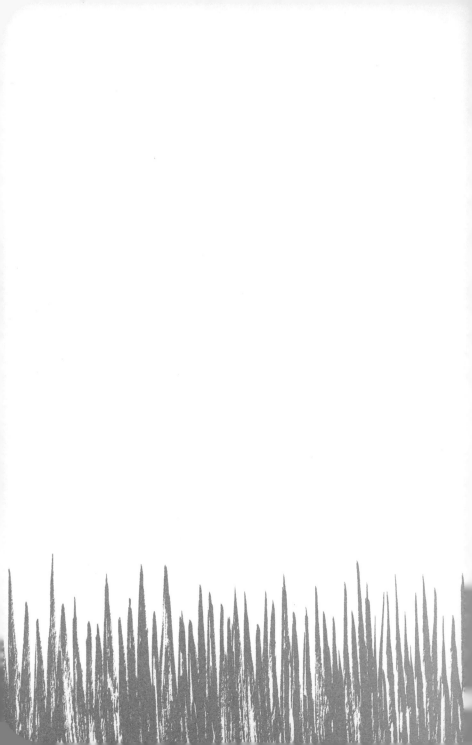

NURTURE YOUR BODY

Exercise is also recognized as a huge de-stressor as it encourages the release of feel-good endorphins into our brains and bodies, helping us feel a whole lot better. We also know that our diet and how much caffeine, alcohol, nicotine and sugar we consume will affect how calm or wired we are.

You might feel like you haven't got time to exercise, or you can't get yourself to the gym or out of the house. Just start by doing housework and gardening. Walk up and down the stairs, clean things, cut the grass and gradually up your exercise regime. You can dance at home to your favorite tracks.

You could get a watch or wristband or app that helps you do more exercise by counting steps, encouraging you to be more active.

There are lots of things you can do to help yourself as a whole, which we will explore in the rest of this journal. Your body and your mind work together, so you need to look after your body in order to be less anxious.

"To live is to suffer, to survive is to find some meaning in the suffering."

Friedrich Nietzsche

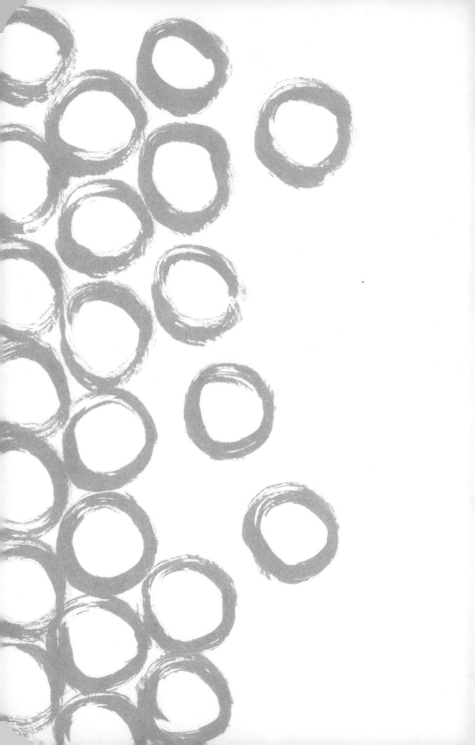

COGNITIVE BEHAVIORAL THERAPY (CBT)

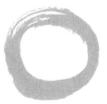

COGNITIVE BEHAVIORAL THERAPY (CBT)

One of the most successful tools for dealing with anxiety is CBT – Cognitive Behavioral Therapy. CBT teaches you to change the way you think, so that you behave and feel differently. It challenges all the assumptions you make about yourself and the world. It teaches a step-by-step method to conquer anxiety and all the feelings and symptoms that go with it.

CBT usually takes about six weeks to learn, but it can be taught over longer periods of time. You can find many courses online, and you can read books (see the Further Reading section at the back of this book).

CBT has been found to be very reliable and just as effective as using medication when dealing with anxiety. However, it is up to you to stick with it. It does take some effort, some determination. You do have to do homework to really make it work for you. Most people report that it is worth it, as the results have really changed their lives.

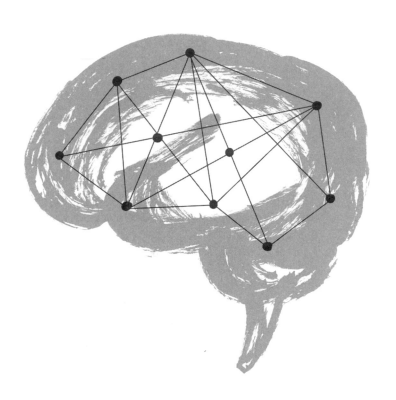

A BRIEF TASTER

CBT stands for:

COGNITIVE – how you see things/events (your perception);

BEHAVIORAL – how you react to events (or perceived events) and how this impacts on your thoughts and feelings;

THERAPY – how you test yourself to change your thinking and your behavior.

CBT: AN EXAMPLE

You have a belief about yourself (cognition) that you can't stand spiders. A CBT therapist would test this by getting you first to estimate how scared you are of spiders (scream! 100 percent!!!) and then show you a spider (or even just a picture of one), maybe at a distance, to get you used to being in the room with one. The CBT therapist would ask you to estimate how scared you are now, and most of the time the fear has come down (say, to 80 percent), as being faced by the reality is often not as scary as you imagine. Eventually, you might get near the spider, or even have it on your hand. In the end, you might have no fear at all. You might have a pet spider!

CBT gets you to face your fears, step-by-step, and to keep assessing how you feel. You can change your behavior (i.e. having the spider on your hand), which then changes your feelings and sense of yourself (cognition) – "I'm not afraid of spiders." This is how CBT works.

By making you face your fears, and deal with the feelings, you can tackle anxiety in all sorts of forms: phobias, obsessions, fantasies, panic attacks (see Further Reading for more information).

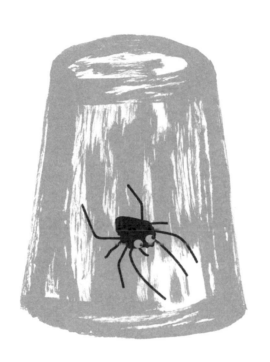

CBT AT HOME

CBT is best taught by a professional but there are certain new habits you can try adopting yourself to ease your anxiety. The key is to distinguish between your thoughts, feelings and behaviors.

Try this ABC:

A: an ACTIVATING EVENT – for example, you have to stand up and give a talk at work.

What has triggered your anxiety today?

B: your BELIEFS – the way you think of yourself (your morals, personal rules, views, etc.). For example, *I can't do this, I failed at school, I'm a terrible public speaker.*

C: the CONSEQUENCES – your feelings, behavior, thoughts, physical experiences, alongside your emotions. For example, you feel fear and anxiety so your nerves get the better of you or you avoid giving the talk entirely.

My ABCs . . .

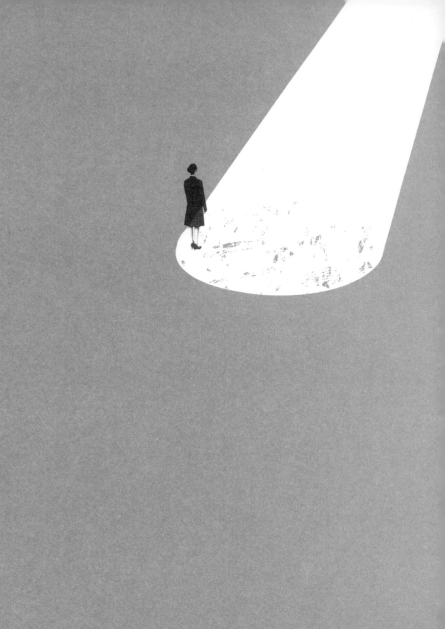

EXPOSURE

CBT encourages you not to avoid what makes you anxious. If you do, you won't conquer your anxiety. In fact, you'll make it worse by embedding it further into your psyche, your habits, your self-image and beliefs.

Instead, CBT makes you turn and face your fear. You face the very thing that makes you anxious, but you do it in step-by-step ways with help, assistance and support. This is called exposure.

Once you face the thing that frightens you, and you see that you can do it, then you can go on to build on that experience and take it further. Using CBT can help you change the way you do things, so you feel differently and behave differently   and, consequently, think differently. You can change how you think by behaving differently too.

CBT can help you put yourself in the driver's seat of your life. However, you have to get into the seat, learn to drive, turn the key and keep the car on the road. It takes effort. But it's worth it.

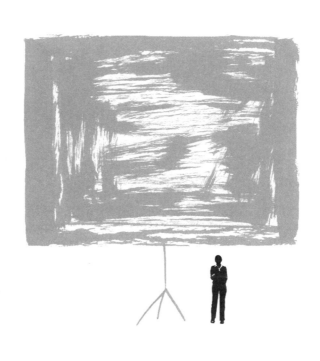

EXPOSURE IN PRACTICE

Imagine you feel very anxious about talking in front of a group. The idea alone makes your knees knock and you shake like jelly and feel sick at the thought of it. The idea is living hell – you feel you'll be totally humiliated and will never live it down. This is your cognitive process.

But your best friend is getting married and wants you to say a few words at the wedding (nerve-wracking for most people). You decide to practice and rehearse your speech in front of the cat, then friends, then try it for real. You get positive feedback. You change your behavioral practices.

On the day, although you are shaking, you manage to stand up and read your speech and you get a round of applause. Before you started you estimated your fear factor at 95 percent. However, when you estimated how you felt after the speech, surrounded by smiling faces and applause, you realized your fear factor had dropped to about 45 percent or even less. You had reduced your fear by facing reality. You tested it out for yourself and lived to tell the tale. It wasn't as bad as you feared. So you feel less anxious.

This is how CBT works. By facing your fears and challenging them, you can diminish them. Now think about how you might implement this system in your life.

NEGATIVE AUTOMATIC THOUGHTS

CBT has a useful model to explain how our thinking works.

Think about a cappuccino. On the top, on the surface froth, are "negative automatic thoughts." These are the surface ideas which bubble up to the top.

The frothy thoughts represent all the negative beliefs we have about ourselves that whiz about in our heads, keeping us anxious. Often these thoughts are self-attacking: *I'm useless* or *nobody loves me* or *I'll never succeed, I'll never get a partner, I always fail, I'm too fat, I've got bad luck again.*

These types of thoughts batter us from within and lower our self-esteem. They flit about and don't do us any good. Most of us have them, and we let them run the show, to our detriment.

What are your most common negative
automatic thoughts?

_____

_____

_____

_____

_____

_____

_____

_____

_____

_____

_____

_____

_____

_____

_____

_____

_____

DYSFUNCTIONAL ASSUMPTIONS AND BELIEFS

Underneath the frothy top of your cappuccino lies the main body of the coffee: a milky mass of "dysfunctional assumptions and beliefs."

These are thoughts and beliefs about yourself that you carry around, which clog up the coffee, making it viscous, and which attack you from within. They are not as accessible as negative automatic thoughts but, rather, are deeper, more unconscious views about yourself or your life.

Dysfunctional assumptions are thoughts like, *Things always go wrong in threes*, or *If I argue with people, they'll think I'm selfish, so I'd better give in, no matter how I feel*, and they can create problems. They work like a self-fulfilling prophecy. The nature of dysfunctional assumptions is that they are unconscious beliefs, often very rigid and controlling, and they support your negative automatic thoughts, like the hot milk in the cappuccino.

What are your most common dysfunctional
assumptions about yourself?

_____

_____

_____

_____

_____

_____

_____

_____

_____

_____

_____

_____

_____

_____

_____

_____

_____

_____

_____

_____

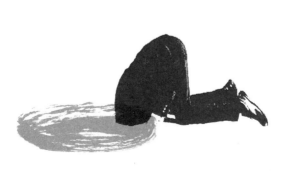

CORE BELIEFS

Right at the bottom of the coffee cup are the thick coffee grounds that represent your core beliefs. These are at the bottom of your dysfunctional assumptions and then bubble up, appearing on the surface as your negative automatic thoughts.

So you might well think, *I am worthless*, *I am unlucky*, *Nobody loves me*, *I'm totally useless* deep down at the bottom of the cup. Your core beliefs are the deeply entrenched ideas about who you are and what you are worth. They go back to childhood and run you from deep down within. Core beliefs are often based on deep-seated negative emotions, such as anger, fear, humiliation, shame, embarrassment, self-loathing, and so on.

Because your core beliefs are often so deeply buried, the way you can get access to them with CBT is through your negative automatic thoughts, which are more accessible. So, tackling the froth is the way in . . .

THINKING ERRORS

When you go away on holiday and think you are "getting away from it all," it is, in fact, still you who is going on holiday. *Wherever You Go, There You Are* is the wonderful title of Jon Kabat-Zinn's book on mindfulness. So, we might think we can escape ourselves, but our mindsets go with us, wherever we go, and bog us down, if we let them.

In CBT these sorts of negative mindsets, which determine your course in life, are called "thinking errors." These are like maps that we unthinkingly follow along particular paths, believing we can only go in that direction. Luckily, CBT challenges us to identify our thinking errors in order to change course – and thereby eliminate anxiety and other negative feelings from our lives.

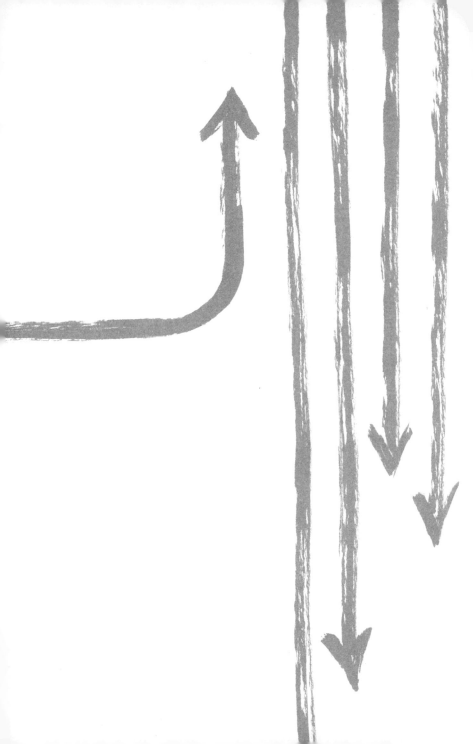

IDENTIFYING YOUR THINKING ERRORS

Do you recognize any of these thinking errors?
Check them off as you go.

1. Black and white thinking: "You're with me or against me," "Take it or leave it." □

2. Overgeneralization: "Just my luck, something always goes wrong . . ." □

3. Mental filtering: "I told you so, I knew it would happen." □

4. Disqualifying the positive: "Yes, but . . ." □

5. Mind reading: "I know they don't like me . . ." □

6. Catastrophizing: "It's all hopeless, the end of the world . . ." □

7. Magical thinking: "Everything happens for a reason . . ."

☐

8. Conditional thinking: "I should be nice to my mother or she'll never love me . . ."

☐

9. Personalizing: "I always get picked on . . . it must be my fault."

☐

10. Blaming and labelling: "It's not my fault, how could they do this to me?"

☐

We can all slip into thinking in these ways from time to time, but noticing and gently amending your thinking errors can help prevent anxiety from overwhelming you. Anxiety is often the outcome of a barrage of negative thinking – so give it up, like a bad habit.

RATE YOUR ANXIETY

How anxious are you?	*You feel…*	*You think…*
Example: You are walking home at night and someone is walking behind you.	Fear	I'm going to be attacked.

Reality check: your fear may make you think you will be attacked, but the person behind is most likely a nice, ordinary person walking the same route as you. It is what your mind does with the event that makes you anxious. That doesn't mean you shouldn't be careful – but you are probably often more anxious than the situation warrants.

Fill in what you imagine you would feel and think for the following scenarios, marking the strength of each feeling 0 –10 (10 is high).

You are late for a work meeting.

You notice a scratch on your new car.

Your child has a temperature.

A letter arrives from the bank.

Your partner says, "We have to talk."

Rate yourself, your first reactions, to each of these examples.
Can you see any thinking errors on your part?

"We should monitor the development of happiness in our countries as closely as we monitor the development of income."

Professor Richard Layard

MINDFULNESS

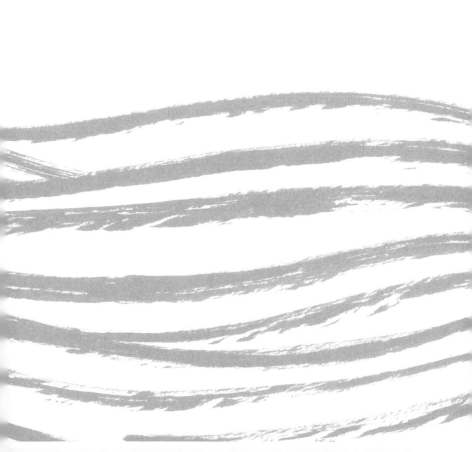

MINDFULNESS

From our speedy, technology-sodden age has emerged a need to find peace and calm in modern life. As a consequence, people in the West have begun to look East to the practices that have endured there for over 3,000 years. Meditation became popular among hippies in the sixties and then developed into a more mainstream New Age movement during the seventies and eighties. Today, people still find that modern science and medicine do not mend all the parts that need to be mended.

Anxiety involves mind, body and spirit. Meditative practices are well known for calming the mind, slowing down the body and relieving a tortured spirit. Increasingly these practices are being merged with existing Western therapies. The practical approaches of psychotherapists such as Freud, Jung and, later, of the behaviorists, such as Skinner, Ellis, and Beck, have helped people hugely over the years. But as life and its pressures have increased their demands the need for something to slow us down has become more urgent.
For many people, the answer is mindfulness.

Mindfulness has grown from Buddhist and other meditative practices. It helps to calm your mind, enabling you to focus on the present, making you aware of everything, in the now. It offers a way to stop worrying about the past, regretting or rewriting history. Mindfulness also prevents you from worrying about the future, for your focus is here. Right now.

TAKE A MINDFUL MOMENT

Stop.

Close your eyes.

Notice what is around you.

What can you hear?

What can you smell?

How does the fabric you are wearing feel on your skin?

How is the temperature?

Open your eyes – notice your surroundings.

Write down two things you see.

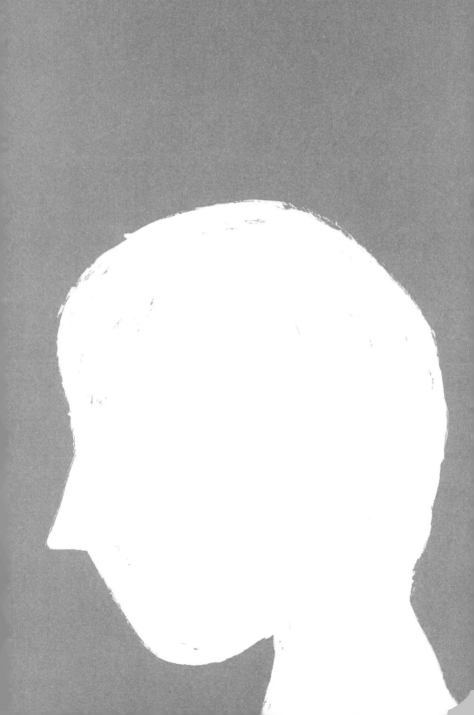

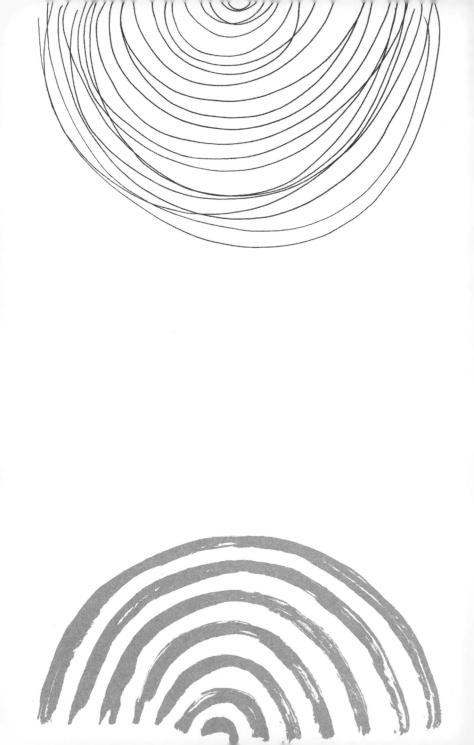

CBT AND MINDFULNESS

Whereas CBT is quite forensic and logical in its approach, teaching you to think and behave less negatively, mindfulness aims to keep you focused on the present moment. CBT is all about mind. Mindfulness is about integrating mind, body and spirit in the now. So a new therapy has gradually emerged: MBCT (mindfulness-based cognitive therapy).

Many practitioners now integrate mindfulness into their CBT work because it encourages awareness and calm, and it is also being introduced in schools, colleges and workplaces to help more people find peace and calm in the present.

The good news is that the evolving fusion of Eastern and Western practices means that we can look after ourselves as whole human beings much better. This is particularly useful if state health systems are struggling to cope as we can become more self-reliant, knowing that we can look after our mental and physical health by calming our minds and de-stressing our bodies.

Mindfulness-based stress-reduction programs have been proven to be extremely effective in reducing anxiety, as well as in the treatment of depression, addiction, pain and illness. MBCT is a practice which encourages you to retrain your mind to operate in a different way. Often yoga, Pilates, acupuncture and other techniques are used alongside it.

BEING RATHER THAN DOING

We tend to emphasize achieving and doing over being and thus put ourselves under pressure all the time. Trying to meet impossible demands is just that, impossible, and yet we still push ourselves to meet every unreal expectation and target.

One way to conquer anxiety is simply to learn to do one thing at a time. This means you learn to focus on what you are doing, in the moment, rather than tripping yourself up either worrying about what you haven't done, or churning about what you have to do next.

Try and focus on the now. Learn to do one task, then the next, and the next. For example, if you're working on a text document on your computer, close down your internet browser and all other applications until you're finished. Aside from the anxiety notifications and windows can create when they ping up, concentrating on one task fully will increase your productivity.

Learn to be, rather than getting caught up in doing all the time.

"I minded not how the hours went. The day advanced as if to light some work of mine; it was morning, and lo, now it is evening, and nothing memorable is accomplished. Instead of singing, like the birds, I silently smiled at my incessant good fortune."

Henry David Thoreau

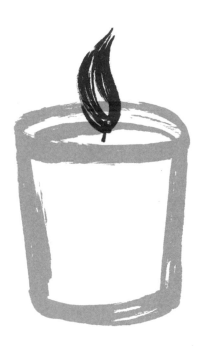

RITUALS

In order to slow down your day a little, build in space to
ward off the possibility of getting stressed or sliding down
into an anxiety spiral. To do this, you will need to identify
the times in your day when you feel particularly stressed
so that you know when to expect your anxiety to arrive.

Are you most anxious:

- early morning, during the rush to work?
- when you're home by yourself, alone with your
  thoughts?
- when you are with a child all day, trying to keep
  them happy?
- during lunchtime, when there is nowhere to eat but at
  your desk?
- commuting in the morning, or on the way back, when
  public transportation or traffic jams seem worse than
  ever?
- during the transition time between work and coming
  home, when you need space, but are instantly drawn
  into domestic chores and family demands?
- in the evening, when you want to unwind but have to
  continue working?
- when you are with someone, and you don't feel you
  can connect?
- when you open your bank statements?
- at night, when you wake up, at 3 a.m., pulse racing?

Your personal anxiety patterns will have their own shape, nature and remedy. Once you've identified your triggers, you can work out what you need to do to change them. What could you do to help yourself during your most anxious time? The next few pages contain some tips that might help.

Did you work out when you are most anxious?

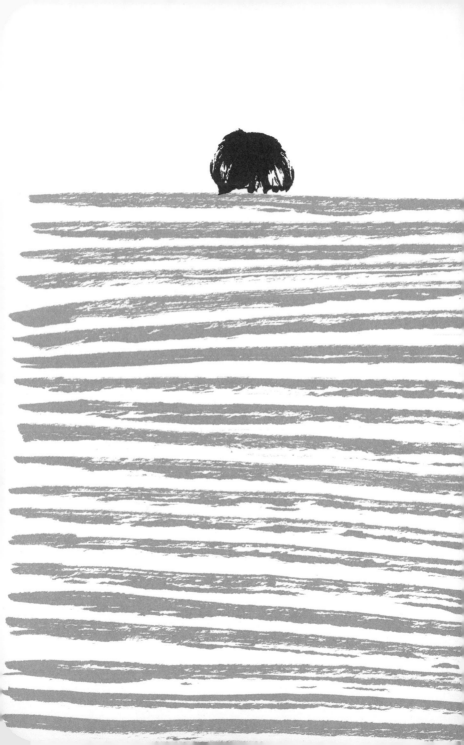

WHEN YOU WAKE UP

Do you peek out from under the duvet and think,
Oh no, I can't face today, or wake up with a knot in your
stomach, or a headache? What do you think about in
these waking moments? Can you catch your Negative
Automatic Thoughts as they fly through your mind?
Try writing them down or, if you prefer, keep a video
or audio diary.

To combat anxiety, you might want to set your alarm
fifteen or thirty minutes early to give yourself more time.
Anxiety often stems from trying to do too much in too
little time or not being organized. Spending time treating
yourself well, and getting ready mindfully, can help you
start the day feeling focused and calm.

Take a deep breath, or several, before getting out of bed.

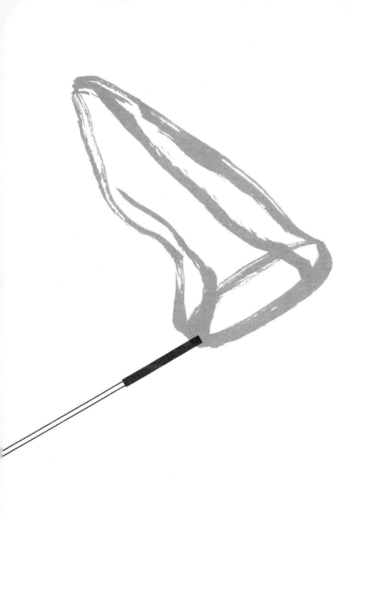

A MINDFUL MORNING EXERCISE

Stay under the duvet. Set the timer for five minutes.

Lie on your back, and close your eyes. Notice where
the tension or any aches are in your body. Now go to
that place in your body and allow yourself to feel what's
happening there.

Exaggerate the feeling, allowing your mind to focus on
it. Then relax. Tense up again and really feel the feeling.
Then relax.

Imagine a huge butterfly net coming along and sweeping
over your head and down your body. All the tense,
difficult feelings are swept up in the net and are taken
away.

Tell yourself, *I can do this. I can face the day*. Take a deep
breath, and breathe out fully. And again, twice.

Open your eyes and calmly pull back the duvet.

You can get on with your day. You are prepared.

A MINDFUL BREAKFAST

If you go out to work, it's easy to leave the house in the morning in a rush. It's also easy to skip breakfast if you've woken up too late or feel you haven't got time.

Try not to leave the house hungry, as you will pick up sugary snacks on the way or end up too hungry to concentrate, walk safely or drive properly.

If you want to lower anxiety, it is absolutely essential to have some nourishing breakfast. It's also important for you to take time to prepare it. The night before, some people soak oats for a nice and healthy breakfast or make sandwiches for the next day. You need, at least, to make sure you have cereal, bread and fruit, eggs, milk, oatmeal, yogurt and whatever else you like, so you have nourishing food to start the day with. If you have a hangover, breakfast and rehydration are extremely important for helping your body to recover faster and enabling you to start the day more focused.

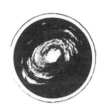

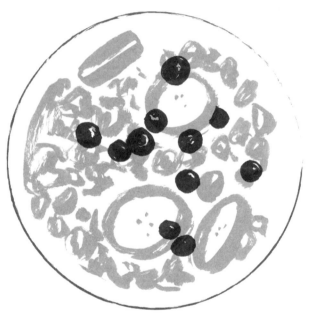

Set a place for yourself and make your table look nice, or at least clean. If you make toast or have a bowl of cereal and fruit, eat it sitting at the table without distractions like the radio or TV, reading the paper or checking your phone.

Just take a moment to eat your food, slowly, tasting the different flavors and savoring the mix of jam and coffee or strawberries and cereal.

You may only sit for fifteen minutes, but by eating slowly, and mindfully, you will set yourself up well for the day.

Eating on the run is bad for both your digestion and your mental state. Slow-release foods (such as whole-wheat toast, oatmeal or whole grain cereal with fruit and nuts) can help you stay calm and energized.

If you are with a partner or have children, encourage them to eat breakfast calmly, if possible. Remember people are waking up. They may be grumpy or stressed or anxious about the day themselves. Avoid arguments over breakfast; they leave a bad taste and interfere with digestion. If possible, clear the table before you leave. At least stack plates, as coming back to a mess at the end of the day will increase your anxiety levels.

MINDFUL MOVING

If you are traveling somewhere by bus or train, take a moment to focus. Look around you. Everyone has got their screens out, heads down. Don't plug in, just take ten minutes to be: breathe, look out the window or just glance around you and observe.

Feel the seat under your legs, your arms on the armrests, or, if you are standing, feel your feet on the ground.

Take a moment to notice the people around you – skin and hair color, clothes, who is asleep, reading, listening to music.

Relax your belly, your jaw, and breathe into your belly button. Feel your feet on the floor.

Take a moment to exist in the present. Risk being bored – a moment of under-stimulation is no bad thing, it will aid your relaxation and improve your concentration on later tasks.

MINDFUL IN A JAM

If you end up sitting in a traffic jam while driving, turn off the radio or any music you are listening to (even just for five minutes). Don't check your phone.

Breathe – take a deep breath and blow it out, hissing noisily. Repeat a couple of times.

Grip the steering wheel hard and tense up and relax (repeat three times).

Lift your shoulders up to your ears and drop them in a big shrug. Repeat three times.

If you are static, put the handbrake on, and sit back in your seat and relax.

If you are alone, shout or growl or sing at the top of your voice. You might even want to swear – get your frustration out.

Open your mouth wide, as if yawning, and close it. Do this three times.

Feel the seat under your bottom and legs, and against your back, and deliberately sit back until the traffic moves again.

If you have a safe way of using your phone, send a message, briefly, so you feel less stressed about being late for an appointment. However, on no account check your phone while driving. It's dangerous and illegal in many states. It will only distract you and make you more anxious. If you're going to be late and it's making you worried, pull in at your earliest opportunity to use your phone safely.

out to
lunch

MINDFUL LUNCHTIME

At work, people increasingly eat at their desks. Try, at least three times a week, to get outside and eat with some fresh air and light. If you must stay inside, move away from your desk.

Although you will want to organize your life, catch up with social media and find out about the news, instead try and take a break from your devices for ten or fifteen minutes, or half an hour, if possible.

Try eating one raisin, or one square of chocolate, for example, or whatever you're eating, by letting it soften and melt on your tongue, without biting or chewing. See how the flavors and textures change. Experience slowing right down as you suck and swallow your food.

MINDFUL AT HOME

If you spend most of your time at home, it can make you feel trapped or anxious, especially if the environment reminds you of all the things you should be doing or haven't achieved yet. If you are a telecommuter or self-employed, unemployed or retired or have a disability that keeps you in, then think about your environment and how you can organize it so it does not make you feel anxious.

If you have children or look after an elderly relative, you may need to have a break, outside, on your own, just to get a "breather." Find someone trustworthy who can give you some respite – you deserve it.

Also, it might help you to have a computer and office tucked away in another room, or behind a screen, so you are not constantly reminded about bills or work.

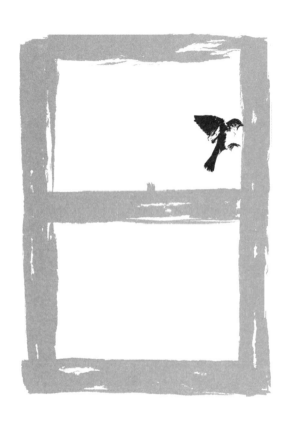

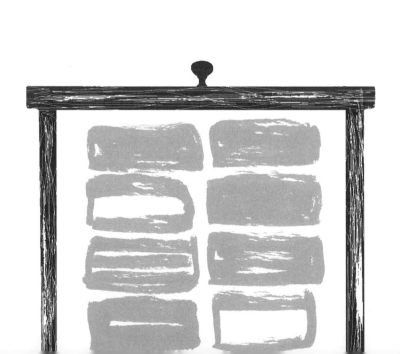

MINDFULLY TIDY HOME, TIDY MIND

Although few of us have the perfect house or household help, a cluttered environment can be anxiety-inducing. It might be that you like living in organized chaos, or you like to be meticulously tidy. Either way, when you are feeling stressed or anxious, it can help to tidy up.

If you hold on to things – newspapers, objets d'art, papers, clothes, shoes – or collect stuff, try clearing a small amount, say fifteen minutes at a time. Amazingly, if you are feeling stressed at home, just tidying one cupboard or one drawer can help you feel better. So take some time to tidy a drawer, empty a cupboard and recycle. This will make you feel calmer and more in control.

Yet we often put off such a task, thinking we have to do the whole job in one go – black and white thinking. In fact, doing a little bit will make you feel you are making progress and may help you to feel inspired and empowered to take on the rest of the job.

Stand back and enjoy your work – your home is now a haven of calm (or beginning to be).

MINDFUL AT WORK

Recent research has shown that many office workers just sift through their emails for most of the day without getting to their productive or creative work. Increasingly, people in call centers or those working in airless, lightless or noisy environments are experiencing high levels of stress and anxiety. There's the constant pressure of dealing with the public and regimented work regimes.

To reduce your anxiety at work, prioritize what you are going to get done that day. Decide what you need to do and make a list.

Look after yourself physically – stretch at your desk, give your eyes a rest from screens, get some fresh air when possible.

Drink water, sipping regularly. If the kitchen's far away and you find yourself forgetting to hydrate, invest in a nice big reusable bottle to keep at your desk.

From time to time, sit back in your chair or even stand up, and move, stretch, shrug your shoulders.

When you feel anxious, sit back and breathe.

Go to the toilet and take a moment to count to ten, tense up your shoulders, then relax.

As a human being, you need breaks – you aren't perfect, so try not to agree to things that are impossible or work non-stop in a way that is harmful to your health.

Have something on your desk or in a drawer that reminds you of loved ones, of home or your favorite activities, so you can reconnect with yourself when you need to.

Remember this is just a job and you are able to cope. Remember you are not a machine.

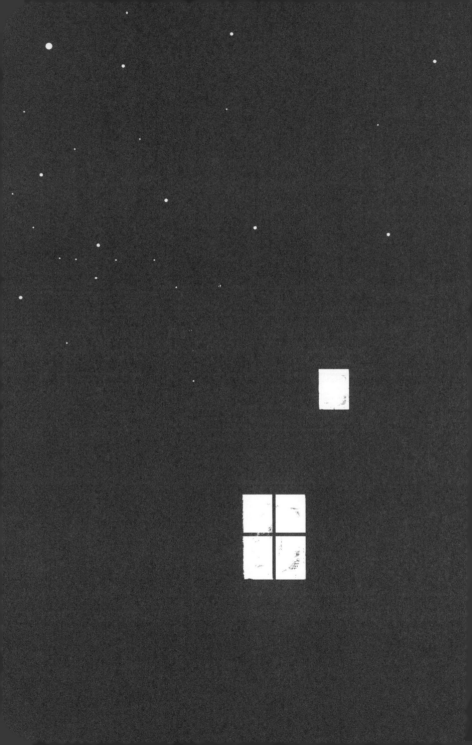

MINDFUL HOMECOMING

Many of us arrive home frazzled. The day has been long. We have picked up tired children from daycare. We might come home to an empty place or a shared house.

Coming home presents a tricky time of transition. It is important to give yourself a little bit of time to arrive home and change into something more comfortable. If you are going out to another activity, give yourself at least ten or fifteen minutes' turnaround time so that you can cast off the stresses of the day. Even if you are coming home to duties and family time, you may need five minutes to adjust – a transition from work life to home life.

If you live with a partner or spouse, you need to negotiate with them that you require a moment to transition between work and home – this is often a time when most arguments start. The children are tired, the home parent is worn out, the work parent is exhausted.

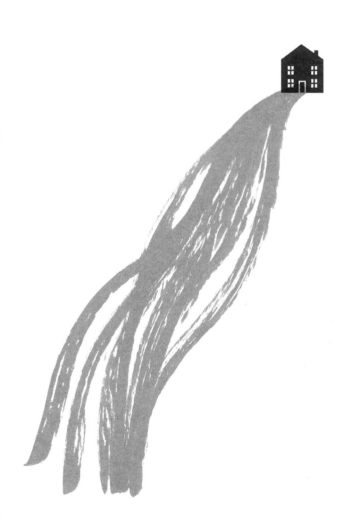

HANDLING CHANGEOVER TIME

Negotiate upfront how you come home with your partner and family. Take it in turns to take five minutes to get changed and calm when you meet up at the end of the day. Take five minutes to be alone before you engage with the household.

Try establishing a homecoming ritual that suits you, so you can be present. Set up what you need with your partner and family – communicating your needs and wishes is all part of establishing a calm, happy home life. Say hello to whoever is there, and then look after yourself for a mindful changeover time.

For example, change your clothes or shower and change. Have a glass of water (no alcohol or caffeine) and don't turn on the TV, radio or computer.

Put on your timer for ten minutes. Lie on your bed or sit in a comfy chair and breathe in deeply. Hiss out your breath, and breathe in again.

Close your eyes and notice how you feel – how do your legs and feet feel? Tune in with your arms, your belly, your chest, your head and face.

Keep breathing and bring your mind to just behind your forehead, and keep doing that for a few minutes.

Continue to feel your body while lying down or sitting in a chair. Notice how heavy it feels and if there are any twinges or aches.

Breathe in again and blow out the breath.

Come back when the timer goes off and take a second to pause before going about your evening business.

Try to also take some exercise, even it's just mowing the lawn, walking the dog or vacuuming. Or you could do something like join a choir or a theater group – anything rather than sitting in front of the TV. Just make sure not to overload your evening schedule. Going out every night, even for wholesome activities, can cause burnout.

Always give yourself some space between activities.

Notes

MINDFUL BEDTIME

If you need to work in the evening, make sure you have some wind-down time before bed to avoid feeling tense.

Limit your caffeine and alcohol intake, if you can, on work nights, as they will make it harder to sleep, and sleeplessness or a bad night will increase your anxiety the next day.

Try herbal tea before bed, or a warm milky drink.

Don't have devices on right before bedtime or LED display lights in the bedroom, as this will interfere with sleep patterns.

It's a good idea to have a warm bubble bath before bed but not a heavy late-night meal or alcoholic nightcap – all these things can interfere with sleep and make it harder for you to get enough rest. This then can lead to an increase in anxiety the next day.

A stroll in the evening air or walking the dog, stretching or yoga can help relax you, too.

Many people find having sex or even just a cuddle will help them sleep.

If you have young children, make sure you work out which parent is going to tend to their needs if they wake up in the night.

If you have noisy neighbors, buy some earplugs so you can block out the noise if you need to, instead of getting anxious about it.

BEFORE BED

Before you tuck in ensure that your bedroom is a pleasant place to sleep in – do a quick tidy-up, even if you're just putting things into piles.

Make a to-do list for the next day, so that you can empty out your mind in readiness for sleep.

Lay out any clothes or get things prepared, pack a bag so you are ready in the morning – all this preparation will help you relax and stop your mind from racing.

Don't listen to the news or watch it less than an hour before bed.

Replace your nightcap with herbal tea or a milky drink.

Ensure a calm sleep environment, with no devices blinking and pinging to remind you of the stress of your work and social life. Also, make sure your bedroom is as dark as possible.

Implement a five-step bedtime ritual. For example: tidy up, moisturize, drink mint tea, take five deep breaths and read a book. In time, your brain will associate these activities with sleep.

My bedtime ritual:

1.

2.

3.

4.

5.

BIG BAG OF WORRIES

Think of having a "big bag of worries" that you can empty your thoughts into before bed or during the night. Write them down, and then you can put them all in, scribbled on scraps of paper – and firmly close it until the morning.

You can look at them in the cold light of day.

Or simply throw them away, unseen.

Whatever, it is important to empty your mind of all the clutter it is carrying.

What worries come up for you in the night?

My worries:

"Keep your face always toward the sunshine – and shadows will fall behind you."

Walt Whitman

FURTHER READING

Change Your Life with CBT: How Cognitive Behavioural Therapy Can Transform Your Life, Corinne Sweet (Pearson, 2010).

Emotional Intelligence: Why it Can Matter More Than IQ, Daniel Goleman, (Bloomsbury, 1996).

Full Catastrophe Living: How to Cope with Stress, Pain and Illness Using Mindfulness Meditation, Jon Kabat-Zinn (Piatkus, 2013).

Happiness: A Guide to Developing Life's Most Important Skill, Matthieu Ricard (Atlantic, 2007).

Happiness: Lessons from a New Science, Richard Layard (Penguin, 2005)

Mindfulness Meditation in Everyday Life, Jon Kabat-Zinn (Piatkus, 2014)

The Mindfulness Journal: Exercises to Help You Find Peace and Calm Wherever You Are, Corinne Sweet (Pan Macmillan, 2014)

Wherever You Go, There You Are: Mindfulness Meditation in Everyday Life, Jon Kabat-Zinn (Piatkus, 1994)

Notes

Notes

Notes

Notes

Notes

Notes

Notes

Notes

Notes

Notes

Notes

Notes

Notes

ACKNOWLEDGMENTS

Thanks to Zennor Compton for inspiration and great editorial guidance, to Jane Graham Maw for brilliant representation, as ever. Also, heartfelt thanks to all of those who have helped me with my own anxiety at Spectrum Therapy, and in particular Vicky Abram, Alegra Druce, Dominic Goldberg, Gill Doust, Tim Davis (for wonderful acupuncture), Katie Smith, Johnnie McKeown and my darling, Clara Potter Sweet, and, of course, the Keedees.

ABOUT THE AUTHOR AND ILLUSTRATOR

Corinne Sweet is a psychologist, psychotherapist and author of non-fiction titles including *Change Your Life with CBT*. A journalist and broadcaster, she is a well-respected figure in self-help and mindfulness is one of her specialist areas (see *The Mindfulness Journal*).

Marcia Mihotich is a London-based graphic designer and illustrator whose clients include The School of Life, Donna Wilson and the *Guardian*.